OUR SOLAR SYSTEM

Pluto AND The Dwarf Planets

Contents

Pluto

Dwarf Planets

If a word is printed **in bold letters that look like this** the first time it appears on any page, you will find the word's meaning in the glossary beginning on page 60.

Astronomers use different kinds of photos to learn about such objects in space as planets. Many photos show an object's natural color. Other photos add false colors or show types of light that the human eye cannot normally see. When appropriate, the captions in this book will state whether a photo uses false color. Other photos and illustrations use color to highlight certain features of interest.

Not Quite Big Enough

What is a **dwarf planet?** Dwarf planets are objects larger than **comets** or **asteroids** but smaller than **planets.** Most dwarf planets are found in the **Kuiper belt,** a ring of icy objects orbiting in the outer **solar system** beyond Neptune.

In 2006, the International Astronomical Union (IAU) created the name *dwarf planet* to describe objects not quite large enough to be called a planet. (The IAU is an organization that names objects in space.) It is difficult to tell whether an object is large enough to be called a

An artist's illustration of the frozen surface of a dwarf planet

dwarf planet. Even with the best **telescopes,** scientists have difficulty measuring their exact size and shape.

According to the IAU, in order for an object to be called a dwarf planet, it must be round or nearly round. It must **orbit** the sun. And it must have so little **gravity** that it is not able to push other objects out of orbit. So far, **astronomers** have classified five bodies, all tinier than Earth's **moon,** as dwarf planets. Scientists expect there are many more dwarf planets in the solar system.

Meet the Dwarf Planets

Scientists officially recognize five dwarf planets— Pluto, Ceres *(SIHR eez),* Eris, Makemake *(MAH keh MAH keh),* and Haumea *(how MAY ah).* All but Ceres are located in the Kuiper belt.

Pluto is the most famous object in the Kuiper belt. When it was discovered in 1930, Pluto was considered the ninth planet of our solar system. But, in 2006, the IAU demoted Pluto to a dwarf planet.

Ceres is the only dwarf planet in the **main asteroid belt,** a region of asteroids between the orbits of Mars and Jupiter. Ceres was the first

Ceres

Makemake

Haumea

object found in this asteroid belt.

Eris is about the same size as Pluto, but Eris is three times farther from the sun. Originally, Eris was thought to be larger than Pluto when Eris was discovered in 2003. And for a time, it seemed Eris might become the solar system's 10th planet.

Instead, scientists classified Eris as a dwarf planet.

In 2008, astronomers classified two more Kuiper belt objects as dwarf planets and named them Makemake and Haumea. Makemake is smaller than both Pluto and Eris. Haumea is about one-third as large as Pluto.

Eris

Pluto

Locating the Dwarf Planets

Most of the known dwarf planets are in the Kuiper belt. The belt begins about 2.8 billion miles (4.5 billion kilometers) from the sun. Its outer edge is about 4.6 billion miles (7.5 billion kilometers) from the sun.

Dwarf planets in the Kuiper belt appear small and faint when observed from Earth. Because most dwarf planets are found in the Kuiper belt, they are also called "Kuiper belt objects" (KBO's).

An artist's illustration of Kuiper belt objects

Pluto was the first object discovered in the Kuiper belt. Many years later, astronomers began to find other Kuiper belt objects. Scientists now estimate that the Kuiper belt has more than 100 billion rocky, icy objects. Some are round or nearly round and can be classified as dwarf planets. Pluto and Eris are the largest known objects in the Kuiper belt. Most of the smaller objects are not round.

In 2008, the IAU created a special category of dwarf planets called **plutoids.** Plutoids are dwarf planets that lie beyond the orbit of Neptune. Pluto and Eris are both classified as plutoids. They are also Kuiper belt objects. Ceres is an asteroid as well as a dwarf planet. But it is not a plutoid or a Kuiper belt object because it is closer to the sun than the orbit of Neptune.

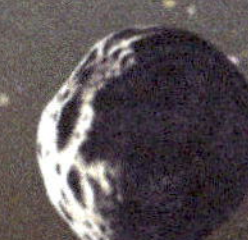

Smaller Than Earth's Moon

Pluto and Eris are the two largest dwarf planets discovered so far. Each has a **diameter** of about 1,500 miles (2,400 kilometers). But they are much smaller than Earth's moon, which has a diameter of about 2,159 miles (3,475 kilometers).

How small can a dwarf planet be? Scientists think there is a limit. That is because all planets, including dwarf planets, must be round or nearly round. To become round, an object in space must have a certain amount of **mass** (amount of **matter**). An object's mass determines the strength of its gravity. Gravity pulls downward on the object's surface. If the force of gravity is strong enough, the object eventually takes the shape of a ball.

Scientists have calculated that an object in space could be as small as about 185 miles (300 kilometers) in diameter and still have enough mass to become round, like Eris, or nearly round, like Haumea. Objects that are smaller and not as round are usually classified as asteroids.

Pluto

is only about half the width of the United States.

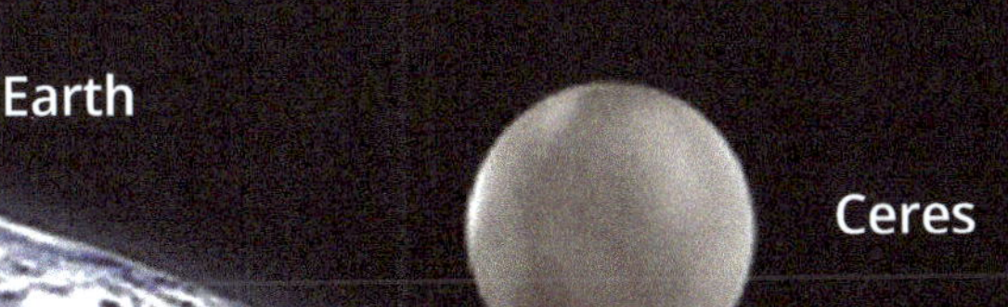

This illustration shows the sizes of the known dwarf planets and their moons compared with Earth and its moon.

The surface of a Kuiper belt object as shown in an artist's illustration

Ice and Rock

All of the known dwarf planets are made up of **water ice** and rock. They have little or no **atmosphere.**

Astronomers often use Pluto as an ideal example of a dwarf planet. Scientists have learned that Pluto has less **density** than Earth. Pluto may have a small **core** of solid rock and some metals. But the core is surrounded by a large layer of water ice. That water ice is much less tightly packed together than the rock that makes up Earth.

Scientists also know quite a bit about the makeup of the dwarf planet Ceres. This dwarf planet has much in common with other asteroids of the main asteroid belt. It is made up of ice and rock. Several space **probes** have studied asteroids in the main belt, including Ceres.

King of the Kuiper Belt

Because Pluto is the largest known object in the Kuiper belt, it is sometimes called "King of the Kuiper Belt." Pluto's diameter is less than a fifth that of Earth. Pluto is smaller than all the planets and several moons in the solar system.

Pluto formed about 4.6 billion years ago along with the rest of the solar system. Scientists think that Pluto collided with another large body early in its history. The debris from the collision formed the moons that orbit Pluto, including its largest moon, Charon.

The American astronomer Clyde W. Tombaugh discovered Pluto in 1930. He spotted it while examining photographs of the night sky taken at the Lowell Observatory in Flagstaff, Arizona. At the time, Pluto was considered the ninth planet of the solar system. But its small size and irregular orbit caused many astronomers to question whether Pluto should be grouped with such worlds as Earth and Jupiter.

Debate over Pluto's status as a planet intensified in the 1990's with the discovery of Kuiper belt objects similar to Pluto. The discovery led to the creation of a new category called *dwarf planets* in 2006. Pluto was assigned to this category.

When Pluto was discovered, an 11-year-old girl from England suggested the name Pluto, after the Roman

god of the underworld.

The New Horizons flyby of Pluto in 2015 as shown in an artist's illustration

A Blurry, Reddish Disk

The closest Pluto ever gets to Earth is about 2.7 billion miles (4.3 billion kilometers). Pluto is so far away that it looks like a blurry, reddish-brown disk through the most powerful telescopes on Earth. Even the most advanced Hubble Space Telescope, which views the heavens from beyond Earth's atmosphere, can only produce fuzzy images of Pluto.

But in 2015, the New Horizons space probe flew past Pluto. Images from the probe showed dark, reddish, ice-free patches at Pluto's **equator.** These patches are interrupted by a bright, heart-shaped region. Scientists think this region is covered with frozen nitrogen. Elsewhere on the dwarf planet, tall mountains made of giant blocks of water ice are capped with **methane** snow.

The dark red regions around Pluto's equator have many craters. Some craters are as large as 162 miles (260 kilometers) in diameter. Some show signs of **erosion.** This suggests that flowing ice is slowly reshaping the surface of Pluto. The brightest regions of Pluto have no visible craters. Scientists think that many craters there were erased by flowing ice. Some images of Pluto show that the dwarf planet may have ice volcanoes that spew a cold, slushy mixture of water ice and frozen nitrogen.

Pluto

AND THE SUN

Pluto's odd orbit is one of the reasons most astronomers claim it is not a planet. Pluto's path around the sun is much more *elliptical* (oval-shaped) than the orbits of the eight planets of the solar system.

Pluto's orbit is also tilted in respect to the orbital *plane* (level) of the solar system. The orbital plane, called the *ecliptic,* is like an imaginary plate. The eight planets orbiting the sun are all somewhat like balls circling around the center of the plate. Because Pluto's **orbit is tilted,** it sometimes travels high above and sometimes below the ecliptic.

An artist's drawing of the frosty surface of Pluto with its moon Charon and our sun

Pluto is

so far from the sun

that it takes about 248 Earth **years** for Pluto to complete one orbit. For about 20 Earth years of each orbit, Pluto moves closer to the sun than Neptune, the outermost planet. That last happened from 1979 to 1999. The two will cross paths again in the year 2227.

From Pluto, the sun looks like a bright dot in the sky. It is as bright on Pluto as the light from a

full moon is on Earth.

Pluto *rotates* (spins) on its **axis** much more slowly than Earth does. That's about once every six Earth **days**. Pluto is also tipped over on its axis, so it

spins almost on its side.

Pluto and Earth

A COMPARISON

The diameter of Pluto is about 1,500 miles (2,400 kilometers). That is less than

a fifth

the diameter of Earth, which is 7,926 miles (12,756 kilometers).

Pluto's average

distance from the sun

is about 3.6 billion miles (5.8 billion kilometers), compared with about 93 million miles (150 million kilometers) for Earth. That means that Pluto is about 40 times farther away from the sun than Earth.

Pluto orbits the sun about once every 248 Earth years. That means that

a year on Pluto is about 248 Earth years,

while a year on Earth takes about 365 days.

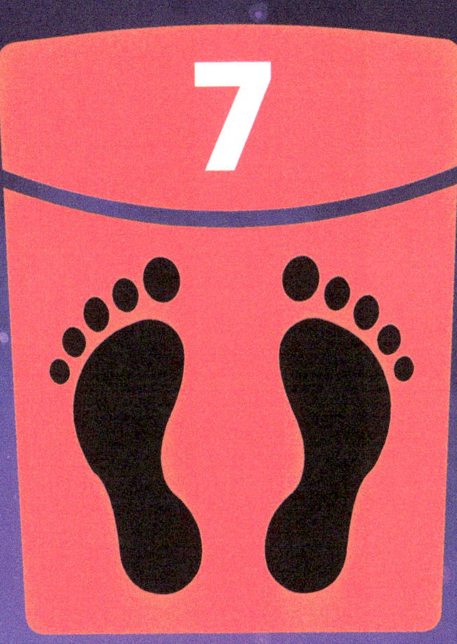

Pluto's gravity

is about $^1/_{15}$th the gravity of Earth. So, if you weighed 100 pounds (45 kilograms) on Earth, you would weigh the equivalent of about 7 pounds (3 kilograms) on Pluto.

Pluto has a

thin, hazy atmosphere

that contains nitrogen, methane, and carbon monoxide. The atmosphere has a blue tint and distinct layers of haze. By comparison, Earth's atmosphere consists of mostly nitrogen, oxygen, and argon.

Pluto has

five known moons

and no rings. Earth also has no rings, but it does have one moon.

A day on Pluto—

that is, the time between one sunrise and the next—lasts about 6 $^1/_2$ Earth days or about 153 hours. That is much longer than a day on Earth, which is 24 hours long.

The Coldest Place

A close-up photo of Pluto's surface taken by NASA's New Horizons probe

The surface of Pluto is one of the coldest places in our solar system. The temperature can range from –375 to –400 °F (–226 to –240 °C). When Pluto is farthest from the sun, the atmosphere freezes and falls to the surface as snow.

Much of Pluto's surface is a jumble of rock, ice, and frost. On Earth, water is the only material commonly seen as ice. On Pluto, many materials, such as nitrogen, exist as solid ice on its surface.

Astronomers have learned that Pluto has a thin, hazy atmosphere made up of mostly nitrogen and methane. Pluto's atmosphere includes layers of haze up to 125 miles (200 kilometers) above the surface. The haze is caused by the breakdown of methane gas by the sun. Pluto's *atmospheric pressure* (the weight of its atmosphere) can be as low as $^{1}/_{100,000}$ that of Earth.

Pluto's Double

Double

Pluto has five known moons—Charon *(KAR uhn),* Nix *(nihks),* Hydra *(HY druh),* Kerberos *(KER ber ohs),* and Styx *(sticks).* Charon is Pluto's largest and best-known moon. Charon has a diameter of about 750 miles (1,200 kilometers). It is about half the size of Pluto itself!

Charon is so close to Pluto in size that the two actually orbit a point above Pluto's surface. This point between two orbiting objects is called a *barycenter.* Because of this, Pluto and Charon are often referred to as a *double dwarf planet.*

Pluto and Charon are also *doubly tidally locked.* This means that the

An artist's drawing of Pluto and its largest moon, Charon

same sides of both bodies face each other at all times. Charon orbits very close to Pluto—only about 12,200 miles (19,600 kilometers) away. It takes Charon about 6.4 Earth days to complete one orbit of Pluto.

Charon was discovered in 1978 when American astronomers James Christy and Robert Harrington discovered a large object orbiting Pluto. They named it *Charon.* The name *Charon* comes from Greek and Roman **mythology.** Charon was the ferryman who carried souls across the river to the underworld realm ruled by Pluto.

Charon

is about as wide as the state of Texas.

Kerberos

Pluto's Other Moons

Pluto's other four moons—Hydra, Nix, Kerberos, and Styx—are much smaller than Charon. The four smaller moons are each less than 40 miles (65 kilometers) in diameter. All are irregularly shaped, unlike Charon, which is *spherical* (round).

Hydra

Pluto and its five moons as shown in an artist's illustration

Pluto

Nix

Charon

Styx

Scientists think Pluto's five moons were formed in a collision between the dwarf planet and another large body billions of years ago. A similar collision between Earth and a large body early in Earth's history is thought to have formed Earth's moon.

Astronomers discovered Charon first, in 1978. Using the Hubble Space Telescope, astronomers then found four additional moons orbiting Pluto. Hydra and Nix were found in 2005. Kerberos was discovered in 2011 and Styx in 2012.

All four of Pluto's smaller moons spin very fast and wobble like spinning tops. Hydra spins the fastest at 89 times for every orbit around Pluto. Scientists believe that Pluto once had more than five moons. At least two of Pluto's moons formed when two smaller, rocky bodies merged together.

An artist's drawing of the New Horizons probe near Pluto. Charon is seen in the background.

Exploring Pluto

Only one space probe from Earth has visited remote Pluto. The United States National Aeronautics and Space Administration (NASA) launched the first space mission to study Pluto in January 2006. The New Horizons spacecraft reached Pluto in 2015. The probe passed within 6,200 miles (10,000 kilometers) of Pluto and within 17,000 miles (27,000 kilometers) of Pluto's moon Charon.

During the flyby, the probe's cameras took detailed images of Pluto and its five moons. It also studied the dwarf planet's terrain and atmosphere. The probe measured gases on Pluto that scientists believe escape into space and give the dwarf planet a cometlike "tail." New Horizons also found that Pluto may have an ocean of liquid water beneath its surface.

New Horizons revolutionized the study of Pluto. The probe gave scientists their first close-up images of the dwarf planet. Previously, scientists could only study Pluto as a dim, grainy blur in photographs taken by Earth-based or orbiting telescopes.

About Ceres

Ceres is an icy body that has been classified in different ways since its discovery in 1801. It was the first object found in the main asteroid belt between the orbits of Mars and Jupiter. Ceres is the only known dwarf planet in that region. All other known dwarf planets lie in the Kuiper belt.

Many astronomers thought Ceres was a planet because of its size. As more similar bodies were discovered, however, astronomers began referring to them as asteroids. Since 2006, scientists have called Ceres a dwarf planet.

Ceres orbits between Mars and Jupiter. That puts Ceres at the outer edge of the *inner planets*—Mercury, Venus, Earth, and Mars. Ceres orbits the sun every 4.6 years at an average distance of about 257 million miles (414 million kilometers) away. Its orbit is closer to that of Mars than to Jupiter. Ceres is about 115 million miles (186 million kilometers) from Mars, and about 227 million miles (365 million kilometers) from Jupiter.

Astronomers think Ceres probably formed from many smaller bodies that collided and stuck together. But scientists think the force of gravity from nearby Jupiter prevented additional matter from sticking to Ceres. As a result, Ceres never grew to the size of a planet.

Ceres is shown orbiting the sun in this illustration.

Ceres and Earth

A COMPARISON

Ceres has **no moons** or rings, compared to Earth, which has one moon, but also does not have rings.

Ceres **orbits the sun** at an average distance of about 257 million miles (414 million kilometers) away, compared with about 93 million miles (150 million kilometers) for Earth. Ceres is nearly three times as far away from the sun as Earth. It takes sunlight 22 minutes to reach Ceres compared to only 8 minutes to reach Earth.

At its longest, Ceres has a diameter of 596 miles (960 kilometers). At its shortest, it is 579 miles (932 kilometers) wide. Ceres is less than one-third the size of Earth's moon, but **13.4 times smaller than Earth.**

Ceres has one of the **shortest days** in the solar system. A day on Ceres—that is, the time between one sunrise and the next—is about 9 Earth hours long. That is much shorter than a day on Earth, which is 24 hours long. One day on Ceres is less than half a day on Earth.

Ceres has little or no **atmosphere.** But there is evidence that water vapor sometimes escapes from Ceres. Scientists think the water vapor may come from ice ejected by impacts with small objects.

Ceres orbits the sun about once every 4.6 Earth years. That means that **a year on Ceres** takes about 1,682 Earth days, while a year on Earth takes about 365 days.

Discovering **Ceres**

The Italian astronomer Giuseppe Piazzi *(joo ZEHP peh PYAHT tsee)* first spotted Ceres in 1801. He named the object for the Roman goddess of grain and the harvest. Piazzi tracked Ceres for several weeks but then lost the object in the sun's glare.

In fall 1801, the German mathematician Carl Friedrich Gauss *(FREE drihk GOWS)* predicted the place in the sky where astronomers should look to find Ceres again. Within several months, a German astronomer named Heinrich Wilhelm Olbers located Ceres.

In 1802, the British astronomer William Herschel introduced the word *asteroid* to apply to Ceres and another object found that year, named Pallas. Pallas is the second largest asteroid in the main asteroid belt. The word *asteroid* comes from a Greek word meaning *starlike.*

Astronomers found other large bodies in the same region as Ceres, including the asteroids Juno and Vesta. By the late 1800's, astronomers had discovered hundreds of asteroids. They called the region where most asteroids were found the main asteroid belt.

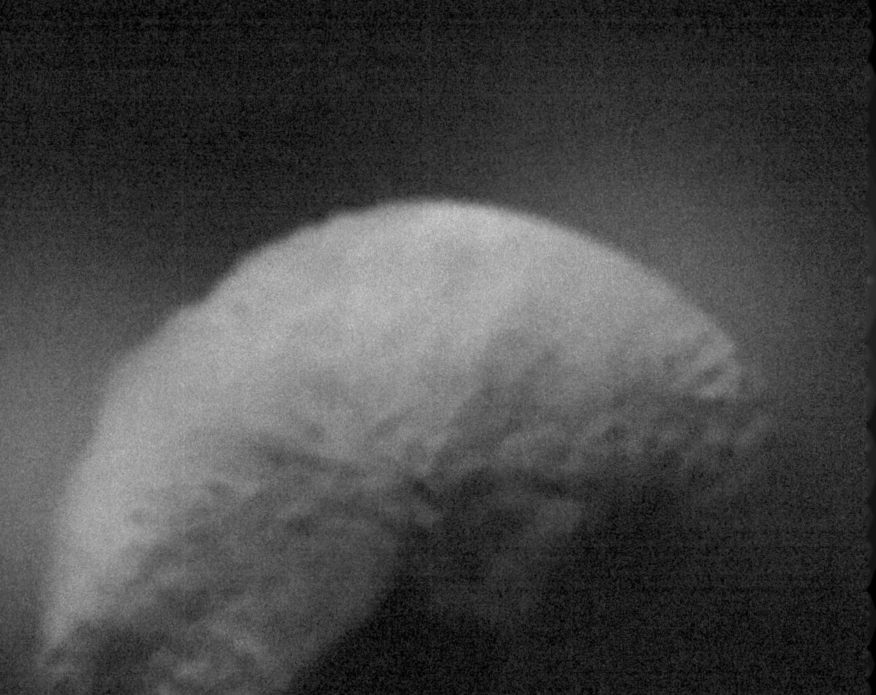

The dwarf planet Ceres orbits in the main asteroid belt, between Mars and Jupiter, as shown in this artist's illustration.

A Dark, Cratered **Place**

Ceres is the largest asteroid and the **only dwarf planet in the main asteroid belt.** Its mass is equal to one-fourth of the mass of all the other asteroids in the main belt combined. Even so, Ceres is less than one-third the size of Earth's moon.

Ceres has a **very dark surface** with several small bright spots.

Ceres's shape looks like a **slightly squashed sphere.** At its longest, Ceres has a diameter of 596 miles (960 kilometers). At its shortest, it is 579 miles (932 kilometers) wide.

Ceres is a

heavily cratered

body. The **craters** were formed when other asteroids in the main belt collided with Ceres. Some of these collisions were violent impacts that ejected a great deal of material from the surface of Ceres. The heat created in such crashes would have melted any ice that existed just beneath the surface.

An artist's illustration of Ceres's dark surface

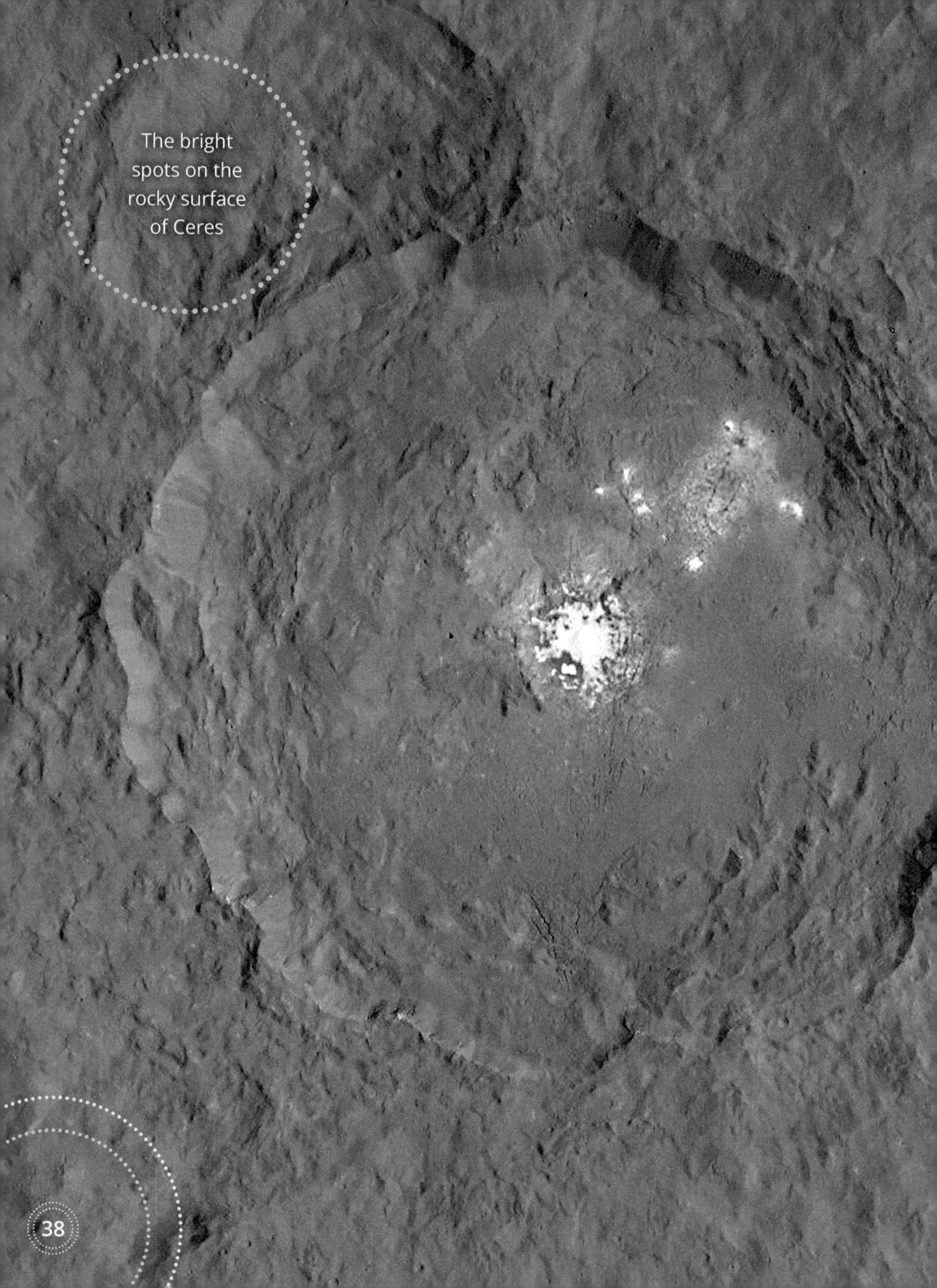

The bright spots on the rocky surface of Ceres

Ceres's Bright Spots

Ceres has many spots that are much brighter and shinier than the rest of the dwarf planet's dark surface. Scientists think these spots are salt deposits on the surface of Ceres.

Scientists noticed that the more than 300 bright spots appear at impact craters on Ceres. Maybe when smaller asteroids hit Ceres's surface, the force of the impact melted a layer of water ice below. Although Ceres has a rocky outer surface, it probably holds a lot of water ice in its interior. When melted by impact, some of this water would be pushed up to the surface.

Ceres has no real atmosphere. When the water reached the surface, it immediately *vaporized* (turned into a gas) and escaped into space. Salts and **minerals** in the water would be left behind. These salt deposits form the bright spots seen on the surface of Ceres. Scientists think that the processes that created the spots may still be changing the face of Ceres today.

Studying Ceres

NASA's Dawn space probe is the only mission that has visited Ceres. In fact, Dawn is the first mission to visit and go into orbit around a dwarf planet.

NASA launched Dawn in 2007 to study Ceres and Vesta, the third largest asteroid in the main asteroid belt, after Ceres and Pallas. By studying these bodies, scientists hope to learn more about conditions in the early solar system and how planets formed. Dawn orbited Vesta from 2011 to 2012 before continuing on to Ceres. The probe went into orbit around Ceres in 2015.

An artist's drawing of NASA's Dawn spacecraft in orbit around Ceres

Dawn made many surprising discoveries. In addition to its many bright spots, Ceres has a mountain that rises about 3 miles (5 kilometers) high on its steepest side. Ahuna Mons is the tallest mountain on Ceres. It has smooth, bright streaks that run down its steep slopes. The streaks may be salt deposits. Dawn also found that Ceres has an interior full of water ice. The probe observed water vapor venting into space from Ceres.

Dawn studied Ceres until 2018, when the probe went silent. Mission controllers think that the spacecraft had run out of the fuel it used to keep its antennae pointed towards Earth. NASA ended the mission shortly after it lost contact. The inactive spacecraft remains in orbit around Ceres.

Distant **Eris**

Eris is a dwarf planet that orbits the sun well beyond the orbit of Neptune.

Eris's orbit

is even more elliptical than Pluto's.

Eris is the

second largest

of the known dwarf planets. It is almost equal to Pluto in size. Both Eris and Pluto are a little smaller than Earth's moon.

When Eris was discovered, some astronomers considered it to be

the 10th planet

of the solar system. Pluto was still widely considered the ninth planet at the time. But Eris was later classified as a dwarf planet along with Pluto and other similar objects in the solar system.

It takes 557 Earth years for Eris to go around the sun once. As Eris orbits the sun, it completes one rotation about every 25 hours. That means **the length of Eris's day is similar to Earth's.**

Eris is the **most distant** dwarf planet. It is almost three times farther away from the sun than Pluto. Eris lies from 3.5 billion to 9 billion miles (5.6 billion to 14.5 billion kilometers) from the sun.

Eris was discovered by astronomers in early 2005. They named the tiny world Xena after a fictional television character. The IAU assigned the newly discovered object the temporary designation *2003 UB313.* In 2006, astronomers re-named the object *Eris* for the **Greek goddess of chaos and strife.**

The sun shining on the distant dwarf planet Eris

Shining Bright
in the Solar System

The surface of Eris is white and very shiny. In fact, it is one of the brightest objects in the solar system.

Like Pluto, Eris is made mostly of water ice and some rock. But Eris has no distinct surface features. In contrast, Pluto is reddish-brown in color, with bright and dark regions and many different kinds of land, including hills and mountains.

Eris reflects about 96 percent of the sunlight that hits it. Pluto reflects about 60 percent of sunlight reaching it.

Scientists think Eris may be so white and shiny because it has a thin atmosphere made of frozen methane. This frozen atmosphere could form a thin reflective sheet of ice.

The surface of Eris is extremely cold. Temperatures vary from about –359 °F (–217 °C) to –405 °F (–243 °C). The atmosphere collapses and freezes and turns to snow because Eris is often so far from the sun. The atmosphere thaws as Eris gets closest to the sun in its distant orbit.

Eris and its tiny moon as shown in an artist's illustration

Eris is so large that all the objects in the main asteroid belt could fit inside.

Eris and Earth

A COMPARISON

Like Earth, Eris has only **one moon** and no rings.

Eris **orbits the sun** at a distance ranging from 3.5 billion to 9 billion miles (5.6 billion to 14.5 billion kilometers) away, compared with about 93 million miles (150 million kilometers) for Earth. That is about 39 times Earth's distance from the sun.

Eris has a diameter of 1,450 miles (2,350 kilometers), about two-thirds the diameter of Earth's moon.

A day on Eris—

that is, the time between one sunrise and the next—is about 25 Earth hours long. That is about an hour longer than a day on Earth, which is 24 hours long.

Eris has a thin

atmosphere

made of frozen methane. Astronomers think the atmosphere freezes because the dwarf planet is so far from the sun, three times farther than Pluto. But the atmosphere thaws as Eris moves closer to the sun.

Eris orbits the sun once about every 557 Earth years. That means that

a year on Eris

takes about 557 Earth days, while a year on Earth takes about 365 days.

Eris's Tiny Moon

Dysnomia is the name of the only moon orbiting the distant dwarf planet Eris. This very small body has a nearly circular orbit that takes about 16 days to complete. Like Eris, Dysnomia is a Kuiper belt object. It has an approximate diameter of between 217 and 304 miles (350 and 490 kilometers).

Dysnomia was discovered by the same team of astronomers that discovered Eris. Shortly after finding Eris in 2005, the astronomers discovered that Eris had a moon. The moon is named after Eris's daughter, the demon Greek goddess of lawlessness.

An artist's drawing of the dwarf planet Eris and its moon Dysnomia. The sun is the small bright star in the distance.

About Makemake

Makemake is a dwarf planet in the Kuiper belt. Makemake was discovered by astronomers in March 2005.

In 2008, the IAU officially classified the Kuiper belt object as a dwarf planet and officially named it Makemake. Makemake was **the chief god** in the mythology of the Rapa Nui people of Easter Island in the South Pacific Ocean.

Makemake is about 890 miles (1,430 kilometers) in diameter, making it smaller than both Pluto and Eris. Makemake also has a **shiny surface** like both of those dwarf planets. It also has a slightly reddish color and may have an atmosphere of frozen methane.

Makemake circles the sun on an elliptical path at an average distance of 4.3 billion miles (6.8 billion kilometers). Makemake is **so far from the sun** that it takes about 305 Earth years to circle the sun once. That is the length of a year on Makemake. The length of a day on Makemake is about 22 hours long.

Like Pluto and most other dwarf planets, Makemake lies beyond Neptune's orbit. For this reason, Makemake is also called a **plutoid.**

In 2016, astronomers announced **the discovery of a moon** hiding in the glare of Makemake. The moon, nicknamed MK 2, is more than 1,300 times fainter than Makemake and more than 13,000 miles (21,000 kilometers) away from the dwarf planet. The tiny moon has a diameter of about 100 miles (160 kilometers).

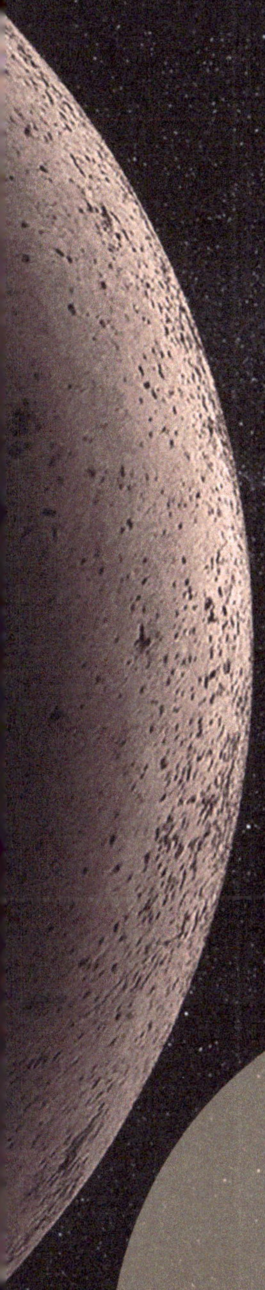

This artist's drawing shows the dwarf planet Makemake and its newly discovered moon.

About Haumea

Haumea is the fifth named dwarf planet and the **third largest.** Only Pluto and Eris are larger. Haumea is a plutoid that lies beyond the orbit of Neptune most of the time.

Haumea has an elliptical orbit and sometimes comes closer to the sun than Pluto. Haumea spins rapidly on its axis. It makes one complete turn about every four hours, so a day on Haumea is about four Earth hours long. That is one of the **shortest days in the solar system!**

It takes Haumea **285** Earth years to travel around the sun. A year on Haumea is 285 Earth years.

Haumea is about one-third as large as Pluto. It is as wide as Pluto but more *oblong,* like an American football or rugby ball. As a result, Haumea is longer than Pluto. It is the **least spherical** of the dwarf planets.

FUN FACT

Haumea has a diameter of about 1,443 miles (2,322 kilometers). That means three Haumeas could fit side by side in Earth.

FUN FACT

The discoverers of Haumea originally named it

Santa

because they spotted the dwarf planet a few days after Christmas.

Astronomers first spotted Haumea in 2003. The dwarf planet was named for the Hawaiian goddess of childbirth and fertility. In 2009, astronomers discovered

a dark red spot

on Haumea. Scientists think this may be an impact crater.

Haumea has a

very shiny surface,

so scientists think it is covered by a sheet of ice. Because it spins so rapidly, astronomers think the dwarf planet is made mostly of rock.

Two Moons and a Ring

In 2005, astronomers discovered two tiny moons orbiting Haumea. The moons were named Hi'iaka and Namaka, after the daughters of the Hawaiian goddess Haumea.

Hi'iaka is the larger of the two moons, with a diameter of 193 miles (310 kilometers). Namaka is smaller and fainter. Haumea's ice-covered moons are thought to be the result of an ancient collision between Haumea and another object.

In 2017, astronomers discovered that Haumea has a faint ring around it. That makes Haumea the only dwarf planet with a ring and the most distant body in the solar system with a ring. The thin ring system is about 43 miles (69 kilometers) wide. It is made up of ice particles and debris.

An artist's drawing of Haumea shows the dwarf planet's thin ring and both of its moons, Hi'iaka (right) and Namaka.

Four known dwarf planets orbit in the outer solar system beyond the orbit of Neptune. This region of space is known as the Kuiper belt. Astronomers believe there are many other round objects in and beyond the Kuiper belt that fit the definition of a dwarf planet.

In the early 2000's, astronomers discovered two large round objects in the Kuiper belt that could be considered dwarf planets. Quaoar *(KWAH oh wahr)* was discovered in 2002. It is roughly half the size of Pluto. It orbits about 4.7 billion miles (7.6 billion kilometers) from the sun. The other object, called Sedna *(SEHD nuh),* was discovered in 2004. It is about three-fourths as large as Pluto. It lies about 8 billion miles (13 billion kilometers) from the sun.

Of course, astronomers have only begun to search the outer reaches of the solar system. Astronomers think that once the Kuiper belt is fully mapped, the number of dwarf planets could top 200. NASA launched the New Horizons probe in 2006 to begin exploring the Kuiper Belt.

In this artist's illustration, the newly discovered planetlike object, dubbed "Sedna," is shown where it resides at the outer edges of the known solar system.

Beyond **Pluto**

NASA's New Horizons probe flew past Pluto in 2015. NASA then redirected the probe for a close encounter with another small icy body far beyond Pluto's orbit. On Jan. 1, 2019, New Horizons flew past an ancient object known as 2014 MU69. The object has since been officially named Arrokoth. The word means "sky" in the language of the Native American Powhatan people.

Arrokoth is the most distant object ever observed by a space probe launched from Earth. Its orbit lies about 1 billion miles (1.5 billion kilometers) beyond Pluto. It is 4 billion miles (6.5 billion kilometers) from Earth and about 43 times farther from the sun than Earth.

An artist's illustration of the New Horizons flyby of Arrokoth

The New Horizons flyby of Arrokoth left scientists baffled by the object's appearance. Photos taken during the probe's close observation revealed that Arrokoth has a red, icy surface. It looks like a flattened, reddish-colored "snowman." Its unique shape consists of two lobes that likely merged together during a slow collision in the early formation of the solar system. Arrokoth is just 21 miles (34 kilometers) long and less than 30 miles (48 kilometers) in diameter.

New Horizons was expected to explore other distant objects in the outer solar system before the probe runs out of power in the mid-2030's.

Glossary

asteroid A small body made of rocky material or metal that orbits a star.

astronomer A scientist who studies stars, planets, and other objects or forces in space.

atmosphere *(AT muh sfihr)* The mass of gases that surrounds a planet or other body.

axis In planets, the imaginary line about which the planet seems to turn, or rotate.

comet A small body made of dirt and ice that orbits the sun.

core The center part of the inside of a planet, moon, or star.

crater A bowl-shaped depression on the surface of a planet or other body created by the impact of an object.

day The time it takes a planet to *rotate* (spin) once around its axis and come back to the same position in relation to the sun.

density The amount of matter in a given space.

diameter The length of a straight line through the middle of a circle or anything shaped like a ball.

dwarf planet A rounded body in space orbiting a star, which does not have enough gravitational pull to clear other objects from its orbit.

equator An imaginary circle around the middle of a planet.

erosion A natural process by which rock or other material is broken loose from a surface at one location and moved to another.

gravity The force of attraction that acts between all objects because of their mass.

Kuiper *(KY pur)* **belt** A ring of icy objects orbiting in the outer solar system beyond Neptune. Scientists believe that many comets are objects from the Kuiper belt.

main asteroid belt The region between Mars and Jupiter where most asteroids exist.

mass The amount of matter that an object has.

matter The substance, or material, of which all objects are made.

methane A compound formed of the chemical elements carbon and hydrogen.

mineral A substance, such as tin, salt, or sulfur, that is formed naturally in rocks.

moon A smaller body that orbits a planet, dwarf planet, or asteroid.

mythology Certain types of legends or stories.

orbit The path that a smaller body takes around a larger body; for instance, the path that a planet takes around the sun.

planet A large, round body in space that orbits a star. A planet must have sufficient gravitational pull to clear other objects from the area of its orbit.

plutoid A dwarf planet that lies beyond the orbit of Neptune.

probe An unpiloted device sent to explore space. Most probes send *data* (information) from space back to Earth.

solar system A group of bodies in space made up of a star and the planets and other objects orbiting that star.

sphere A round, ball-shaped object.

telescope An instrument for making distant objects appear nearer and larger. Simple telescopes usually consist of an arrangement of lenses, and sometimes mirrors, in one or more tubes.

water ice A term scientists use to describe frozen water, to distinguish it from ice that forms from other chemical substances.

year The time it takes a planet to complete one orbit around the sun.

Index

Q

R

S

T

V

W

Y

World Book, Inc.
180 North LaSalle Street
Suite 900
Chicago, Illinois 60601
USA

For information about other "Solar System" titles, as well as other World Book print and digital publications, please go to www.worldbook.com or call 1-800-WORLDBK (967-5325).

For information about sales to schools and libraries, call 1-800-975-3250 (United States) or 1-800-837-5365 (Canada).

Library of Congress Cataloging-in-Publication Data for this volume has been applied for.

Our Solar System
ISBN: 978-0-7166-8058-1 (set, hc.)

Pluto and the Dwarf Planets
ISBN: 978-0-7166-8066-6 (hc.)

Also available as:
ISBN: 978-0-7166-8076-5 (e-book)

2nd printing September 2021

Staff

Editorial

Writer
Mellonee Carrigan

Manager, New Product
Nicholas Kilzer

Senior Editor
Shawn Brennan

Editor
Will Adams

Proofreader
Nathalie Strassheim

Manager, Indexing Services
David Pofelski

Graphics and Design

Senior Visual Communications Designer
Melanie Bender

Media Editor
Rosalia Bledsoe

Acknowledgments

Cover: © Aphelleon/Shutterstock; © Diego Barucco, Shutterstock; © Elena11/Shutterstock
1 © Diego Barucco, Shutterstock; © Elena11/Shutterstock
2-3 NASA/JHU APL/SwRI/Alex Parker; © Nostalgia for Infinity/Shutterstock
4-7 © Shutterstock
8-9 © Chris Butler, Science Source
10-11 © UCAR/University of Michigan
12-13 NASA/JPL-Caltech/T. Pyle (SSC)
14-17 © Shutterstock
18-19 NASA/Southwest Research Institute/Alex Parker
20-21 © Shutterstock; NASA
22-23 NASA/Johns Hopkins University Applied Physics Laboratory/Southwest Research Institute
24-25 © HYPERSPHERE/Science Photo Library/Getty Images
26-27 © Mark Garlick, Science Source
28-29 © Dotted Yeti/Shutterstock
30-31 © Mark Garlick, Science Photo Library/Getty Images
32-33 © Shutterstock; NASA
34-35 NASA/ESA/ATG medialab
36-37 © Mark Garlick, Science Photo Library/Getty Images
38-41 NASA/JPL-Caltech/UCLA/MPS/DLR/IDA
42-43 © Andamati/Shutterstock
44-45 NASA/ESA/STScI
46-47 © Shutterstock; NASA
48-49 NASA/JPL-Caltech
50-51 NASA/ESA/A. Parker (Southwest Research Institute)
52-53 © Diego Barucco, Shutterstock
54-55 © Mark Garlick, Science Photo Library/Getty Images
56-57 NASA/JPL-Caltech
58-59 NASA/Johns Hopkins University Applied Physic Laboratory/Southwest Research Institute/Stev Gribben

www.ingramcontent.com/pod-product-compliance
Ingram Content Group UK Ltd.
Pitfield, Milton Keynes, MK11 3LW, UK
UKHW061955290726
14090UKWH00021B/1243